A Dorling Kindersley Book

Project Editor Laura Buller
Editor Bridget Hopkinson
Art Editor Christopher Howson
Production Catherine Semark
Photography Pete Gardner

First published in Great Britain in 1992 by Dorling Kindersley Publishers Limited, 9 Henrietta Street, London WC2E 8PS

A CIP catalogue record for this book is available from the British Library

ISBN 0-86318-795-1

Reproduced in Hong Kong by Bright Arts
Printed in Belgium by Proost

MY SCIENCE BOOK OF MOVEMENT

Written by
Neil Ardley

Dorling Kindersley
London • New York • Stuttgart

What is movement?

The world around you is on the move. People walk and run, animals swim, fly, leap, and crawl, winds blow, rivers rush, and machines race and whirr. It takes a force – a push or a pull – to get something moving, and another force to make it change direction or stop. People and animals have muscles that produce the force they need to move, while machines are powered by engines or motors.

On a roll
Objects move more easily on wheels. If you ride a skateboard, you can travel faster than your legs can carry you.

Catch a wave
Air and water are constantly moving. With a sail and a board, you can catch the wind and zoom across the waves.

Water jump
This salmon is leaping up a waterfall as it travels upstream to breed. Animals also move to find food and escape from enemies.

On the tracks
High-speed trains have powerful engines that make them the fastest land transport.

Fast mover
A hummingbird can move its wings as fast as 80 times a second.

Get a move on!
Moving objects need a supply of energy. This walking robot is powered by a motor that uses energy from a battery. People get energy from the food they eat.

On the ball
When you play an energetic game like basketball, your muscles provide the force you need to run, leap, and shoot baskets.

⚠ This sign means **take care.** You should ask an adult to help you with this step of the experiment.

Be a safe scientist
Follow all the instructions and always be careful, especially when using scissors, knives, glass, or heavy objects. Never put anything in your mouth or eyes. When a step in an experiment requires you to swing things around or shoot them into the air, do it outside, in the open, away from other people.

Lift off !

Shoot a cup into the air and see how high it flies before it stops and falls down. You can find out how objects need a force to start them moving, and a force to make them slow down and stop.

You will need:

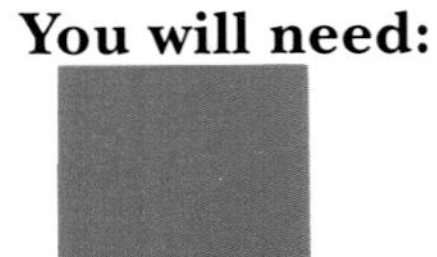

Tissue paper

Empty washing-up liquid bottle

Plastic cup

Water

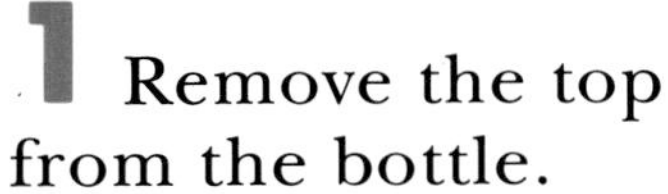

1 Remove the top from the bottle.

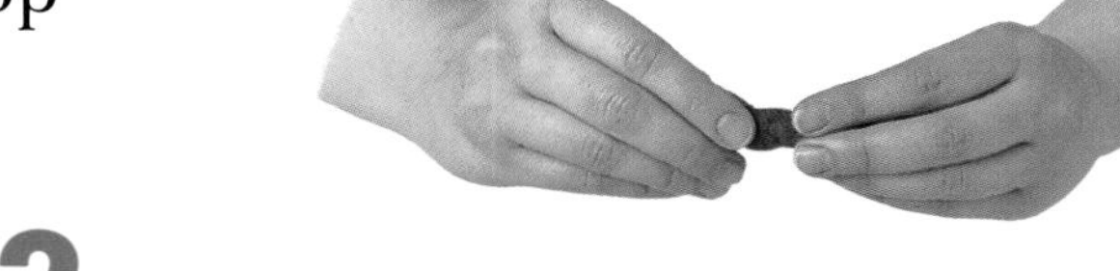

2 Dip the tissue paper into the water and squeeze it into a plug shape.

The plug must fit firmly.

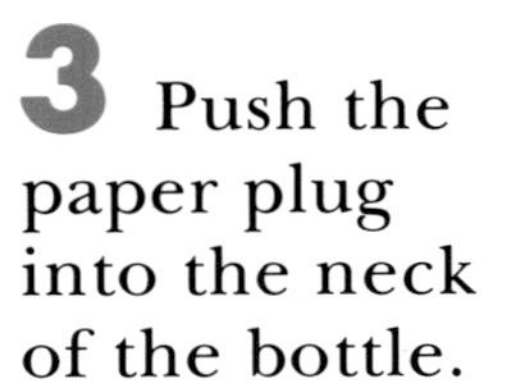

3 Push the paper plug into the neck of the bottle.

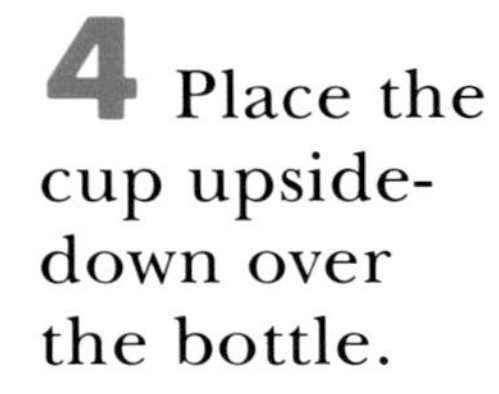

4 Place the cup upside-down over the bottle.

The force of gravity pulls down on the cup, slowing it to a stop, then making the cup fall back down.

The force of the air in the bottle makes the plug move. The force of the moving plug then lifts the cup.

5 Point the bottle into an open space. Squeeze it hard with both hands. The cup shoots into the air, then stops, and falls down.

Squeezing the bottle makes the air inside push against the plug with a strong force.

Fiery flight
A space rocket lifts off as its engines fire. Burning fuel in the engines produces a powerful force that makes the rocket move upwards.

Swerve and score

Make your own pin-ball game. To get the balls to go through all the holes, you will need to find out how force makes moving objects change direction.

You will need:

Magnet

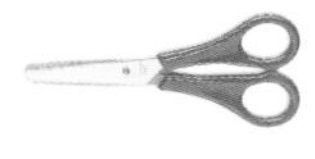

Scissors

Colouring pens

Cardboard box lid

Strip of card

Steel ball bearings

Sticky tape

Ruler

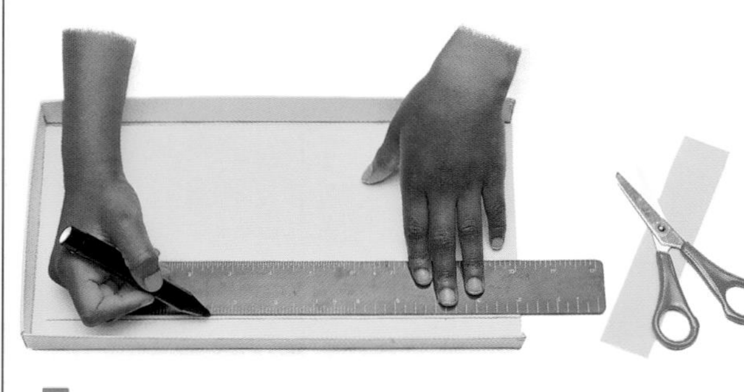

1 Cut off one of the short sides of the lid. Then rule a line along one long side of the lid.

Put the short side against the lid. Cut the first hole where it meets the line.

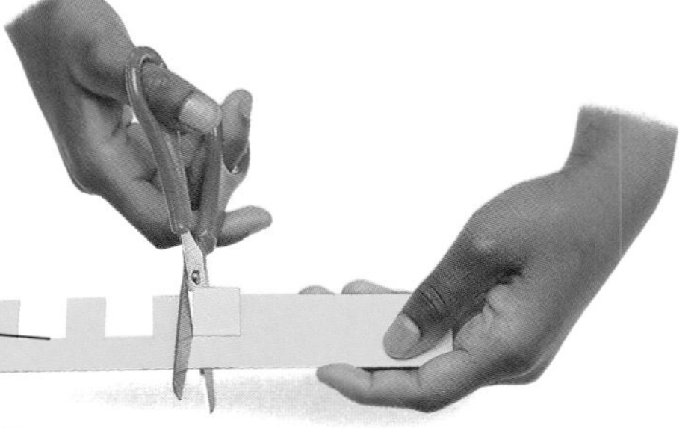

2 Cut several square holes in the short side that you have cut off.

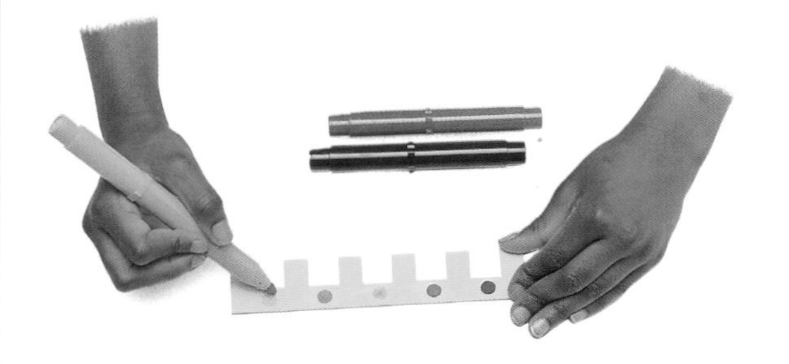

3 Mark the holes with different colours. Then tape the short side back to the lid.

4 Fold the strip of card twice to make a chute. Tape it to the lid over the straight line.

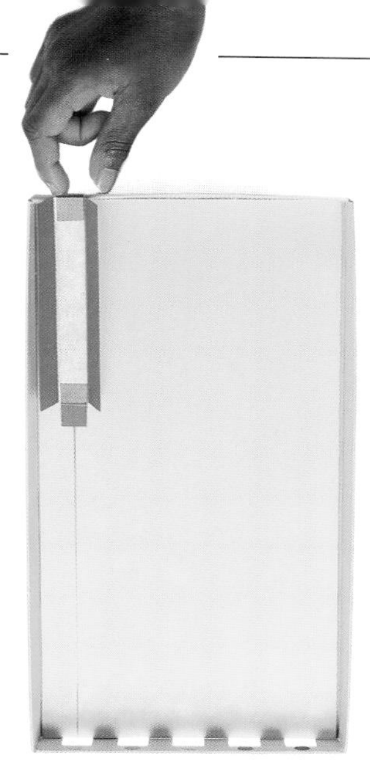

5 Put the lid on a level surface. Roll a ball bearing down the chute. It should roll along the line and go through the first hole.

The force of gravity pulls the ball bearing down the chute. With nothing to change its direction, it keeps going in a straight line.

The magnet has a magnetic force. It pulls each ball bearing to one side, making it change direction.

6 Put the magnet near the end of the chute. Roll down another ball bearing. It swerves to one side and goes through a different hole.

By moving the magnet, you can make the ball bearings go through all the holes.

Pulling strings

A parachute usually drops straight down to the ground. But the force of a wind can blow it to one side. Pulling the strings of the parachute controls the direction of its descent.

Faster and faster

Fill a truck with marbles and see how it moves with different loads. The same force makes the truck move faster when it is lighter and slower when it is heavier.

You will need:

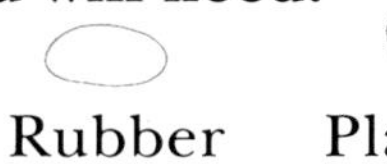
Rubber band

Plasticine

Toy truck

Paper strip

Marbles

Two cotton reels

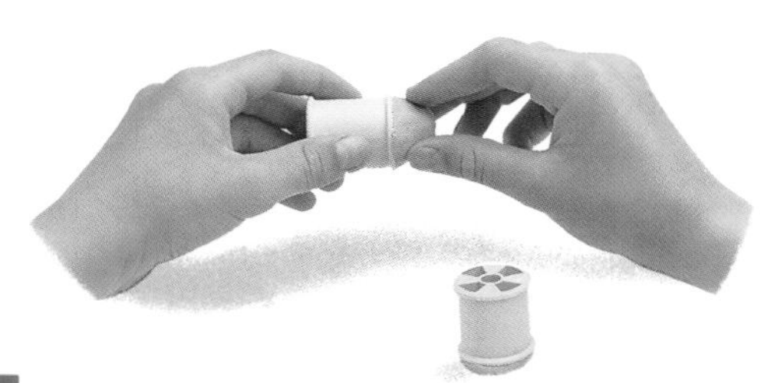

1 Stick some plasticine to the base of each cotton reel.

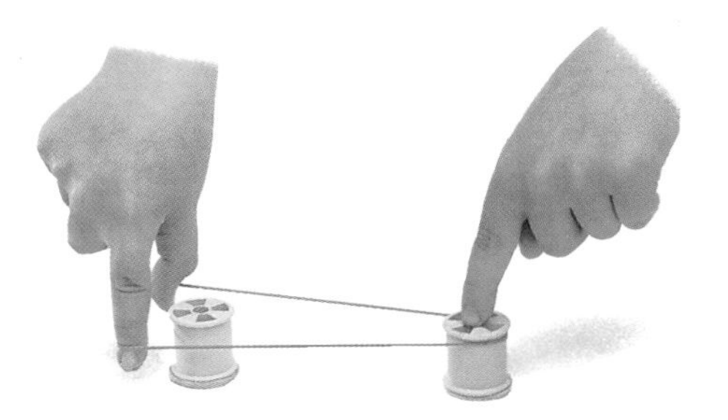

2 Fix the reels to a table top. Stretch the rubber band over the reels.

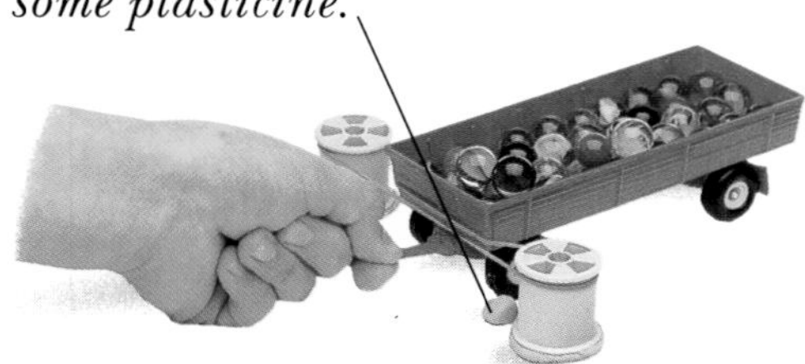
Mark the position of the rubber band with some plasticine.

3 Fill the truck with marbles. Place it against the rubber band and pull the truck back a short distance.

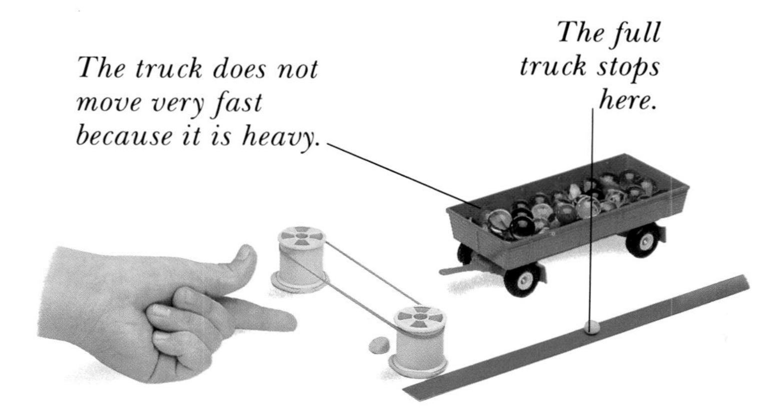
The truck does not move very fast because it is heavy.

The full truck stops here.

4 Let go of the truck. It moves off and travels a short distance. Mark the place where it stops with plasticine.

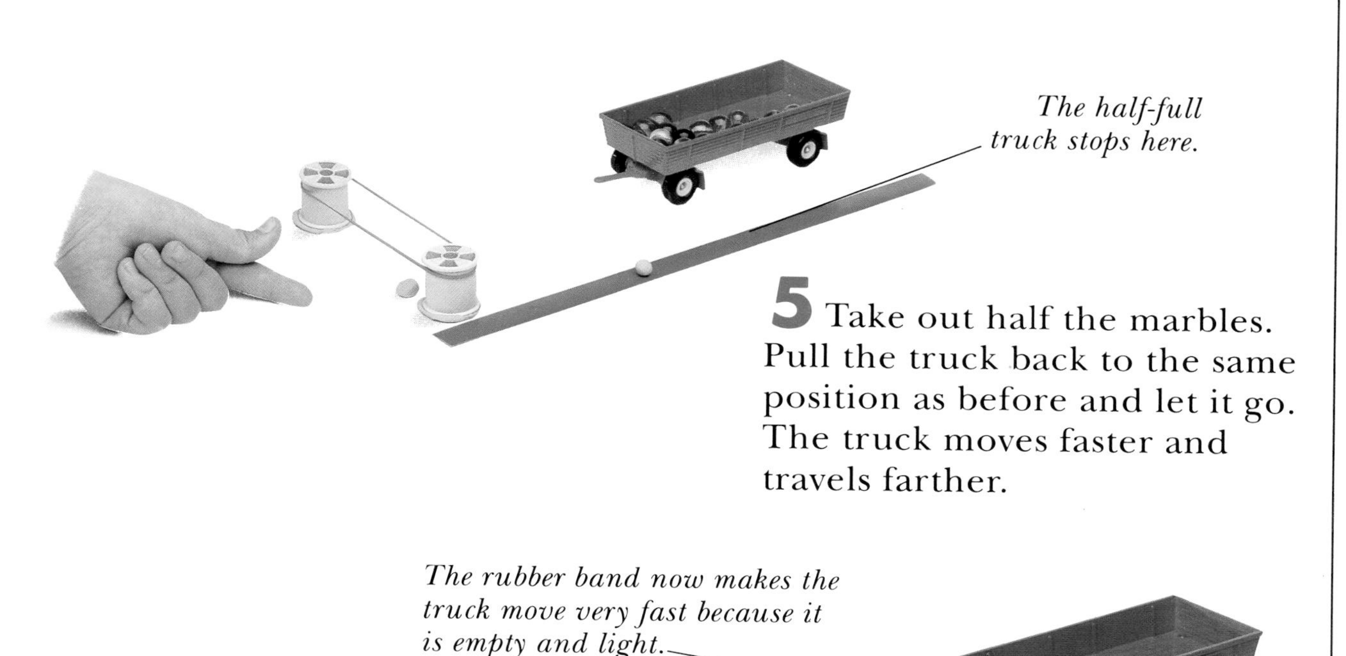

The half-full truck stops here.

5 Take out half the marbles. Pull the truck back to the same position as before and let it go. The truck moves faster and travels farther.

The rubber band now makes the truck move very fast because it is empty and light.

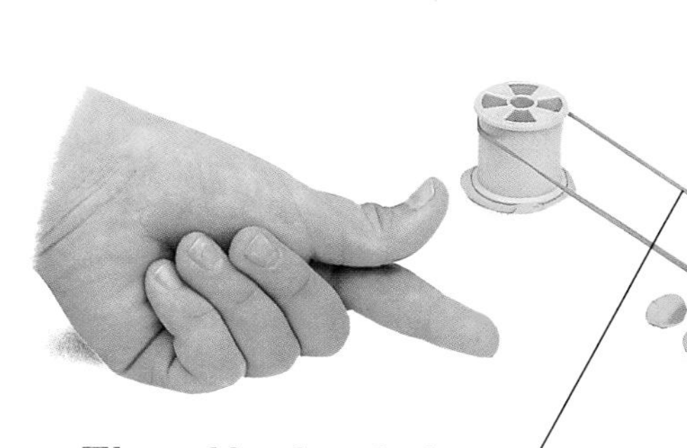

The rubber band always produces the same force to get the truck moving.

6 Remove all the marbles and try again. Now the truck moves very fast and travels a long way.

Pass the puck

Ice hockey is a fast sport. The small, rubber puck shoots across the ice as the players hit it with their sticks. The puck moves fast because it is a light object and the players strike it with a lot of force.

Lazy button

Can you move a card without disturbing a button placed on it? Try this trick. It shows that objects have "inertia", which makes them hard to move. Heavy objects have more inertia than light objects.

You will need:

Large button

Card

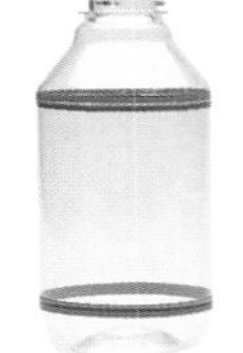

Open bottle

1 Place the card on top of the bottle. Put the button on the card over the mouth of the bottle.

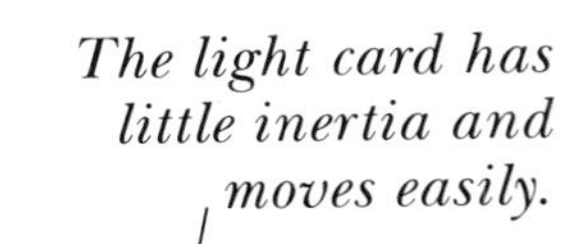

The light card has little inertia and moves easily.

2 Flick the card sharply. It flies off, but the button falls into the bottle!

The heavy button has more inertia and does not fly off.

A big shot
Shot putters need to be very strong. The shot is a heavy, metal ball with a lot of inertia. It takes a big push to make it move away and fly through the air.

In a spin

Try to stop a spinning egg. It's not as easy as you might think. Once an object is moving, inertia also makes it hard to stop.

You will need:

Fresh egg

ırge bowl

1 Place the egg in the bowl. Twist the egg to get it spinning.

2 Grasp the egg gently with the tips of your fingers to stop it spinning.

3 Quickly let go of the egg. It starts to spin again!

When you spin the egg, the liquid inside it starts to move too.

When you stop the egg, inertia keeps the liquid spinning. This starts the whole egg turning again.

Over the top!
This horse has refused to jump the fence. The horse stops suddenly, and the rider flies forwards because his inertia makes him keep moving.

Paddle power

Build a paddle-boat and watch it move through water under its own power. You can see how self-powered vehicles have to push backwards in order to move forwards.

You will need:

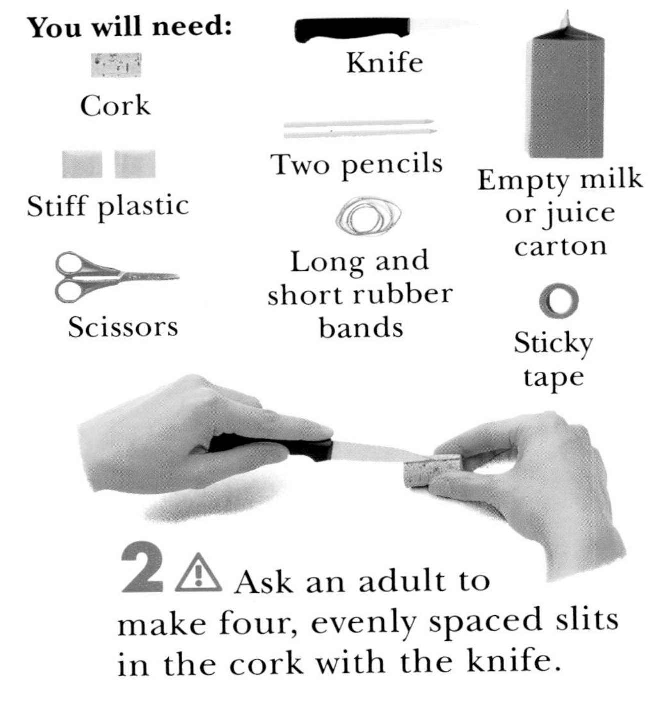

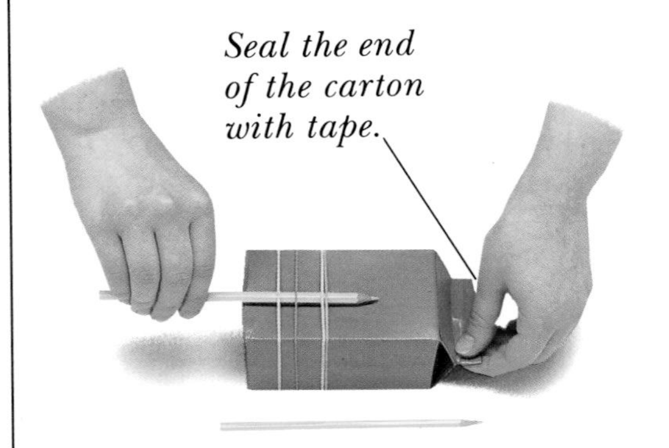

Seal the end of the carton with tape.

1 Fix the pencils to the sides of the carton with several long rubber bands.

2 ⚠ Ask an adult to make four, evenly spaced slits in the cork with the knife.

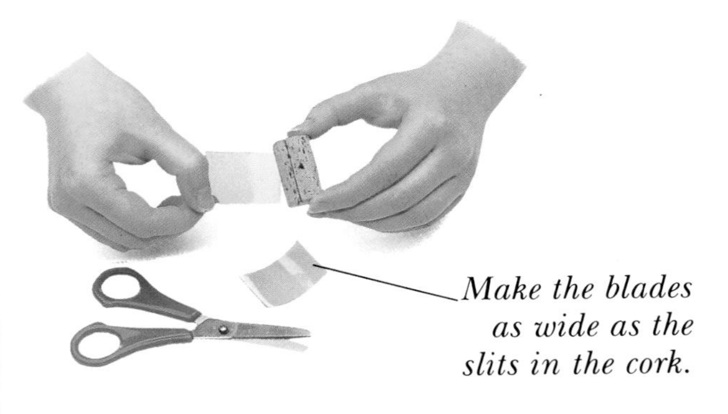

Make the blades as wide as the slits in the cork.

3 Cut two blades from the plastic. Fit the blades into opposite slits in the cork to make a paddle-wheel.

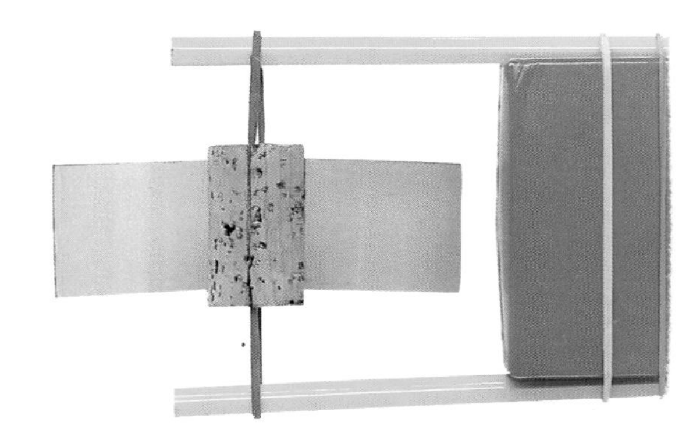

4 Fit a short rubber band into the other slits in the cork, then stretch the rubber band around the pencils.

The sharp end helps the boat to cut through the water.

5 Wind the paddle-wheel, put the boat in water and let it go. The boat travels across the water, powered by the paddle-wheel.

The paddle-wheel turns as the rubber band unwinds.

The blades push the water backwards as the paddle-wheel turns. This action pushes the boat forwards.

Cruising down the river
An engine powers the large paddle-wheel that pushes this great river-boat through the water. Other kinds of boats have underwater propellers. Like paddle-wheels, propellers drive boats by pushing water backwards.

Finger pool

Build a pool table and play finger pool with a friend. See how one draught can make another move using "kinetic" energy. All moving objects have kinetic energy.

You will need:

Four white draughts

Three black draughts

Scissors

Red colouring pen

Sticky tape

Large piece of card

Ruler

Score lines between the corners.

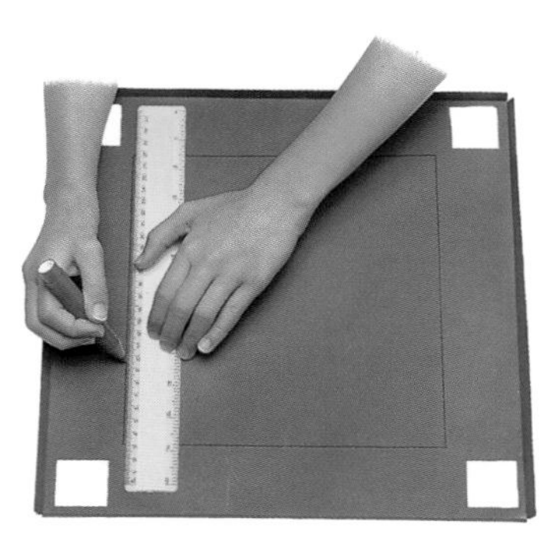

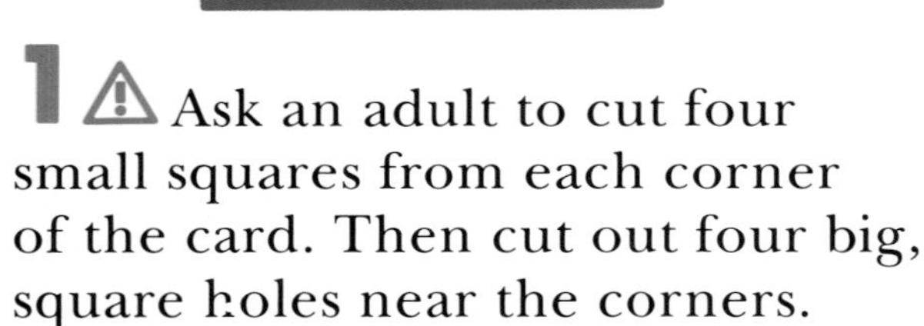

1 ⚠ Ask an adult to cut four small squares from each corner of the card. Then cut out four big, square holes near the corners.

2 Draw a thick red line just inside the holes.

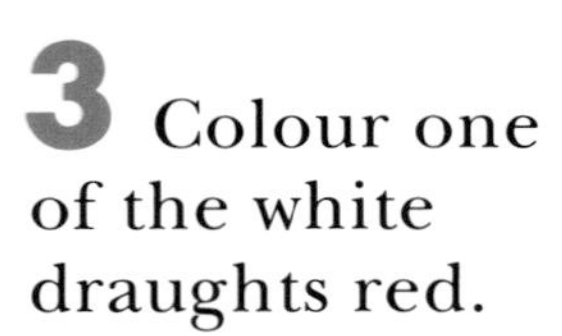

3 Colour one of the white draughts red.

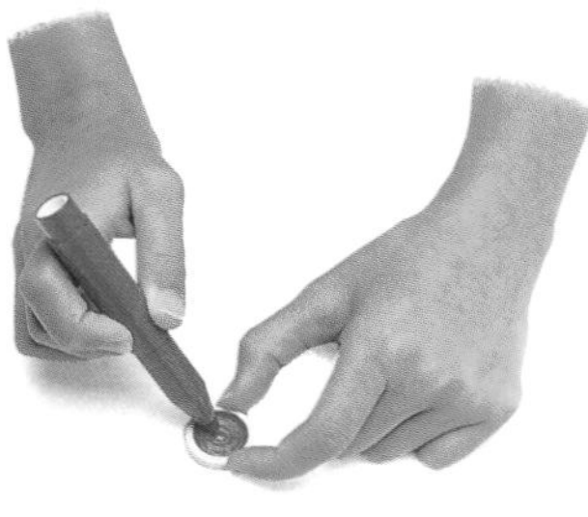

4 Fold up the sides of the card and tape the corners together. This is your pool table. Stand it on a box.

Put the red draught anywhere outside the red line.

5 Place the black and white draughts in a triangle in the centre of the table.

The red draught gets kinetic energy from your finger. It stops as it loses this energy.

Return the red draught anywhere outside the red line after each shot.

A black or white draught gets kinetic energy from the red draught and starts to move.

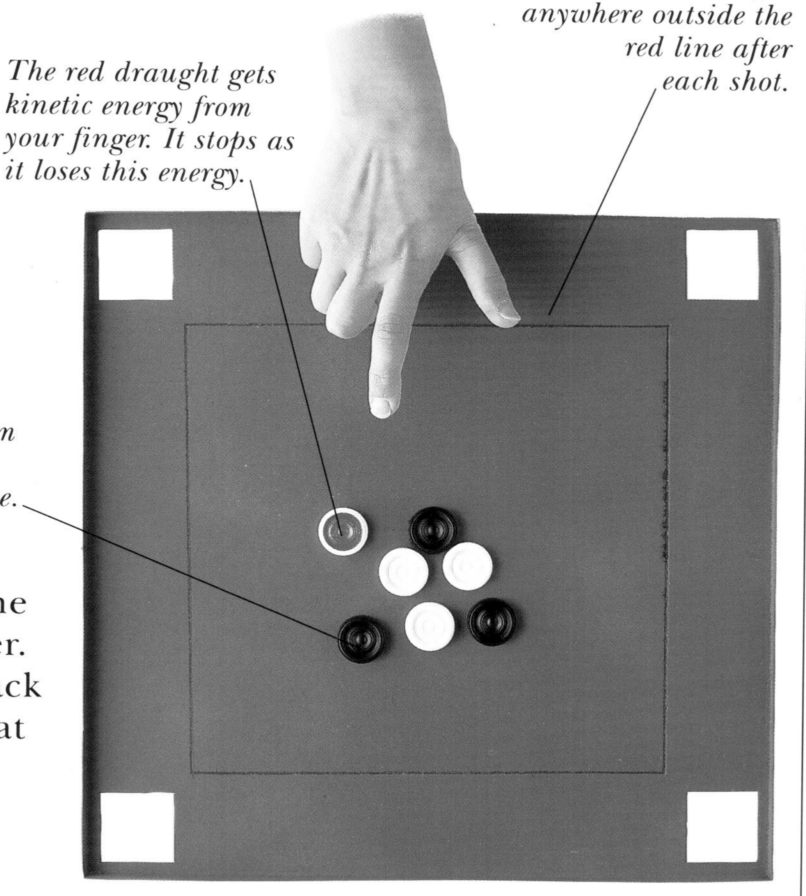

6 Take turns to flick the red draught with a finger. Aim to hit either the black or white draughts, so that they fall into the holes.

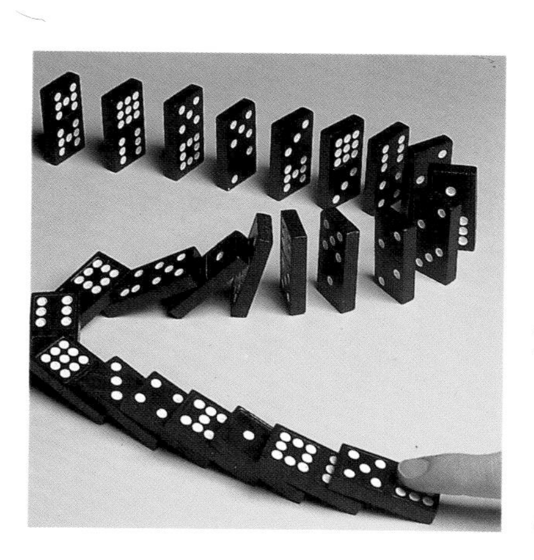

All fall down

You can topple a whole line of dominoes just by pushing the first one. Kinetic energy transfers from one domino to another, until all the dominoes in the line have fallen over.

On the level

Use "friction" to help you perform an amazing balancing trick. Friction is a force that slows or stops movement. There is friction between objects where they press or rub together.

You will need:

Smooth length of wood

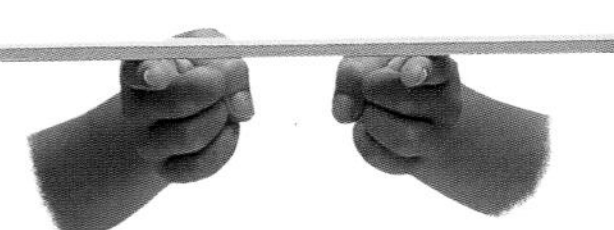

1 Hold your hands a short distance apart. Balance the length of wood on your two index fingers.

The weight of this half of the wood presses on your finger. It creates friction, which stops your finger moving under the wood.

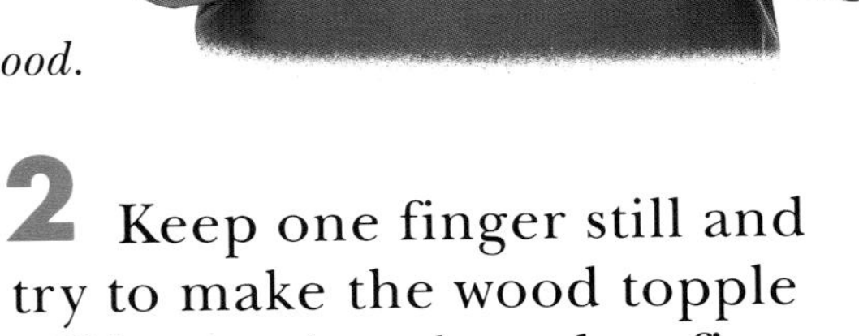

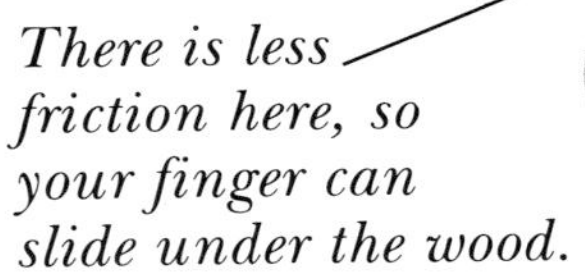

There is less friction here, so your finger can slide under the wood.

2 Keep one finger still and try to make the wood topple off by moving the other finger along. It's almost impossible! Your fingers always end up in the middle.

Non-slip slope

You can often stand on a slope without slipping. This is because your weight produces friction between your feet and the slope.

On the slide

Make a slide to test for friction and see how some objects move more easily than others. This is because their surfaces create different amounts of friction with the surface of the slide.

You will need:

Pumice stone

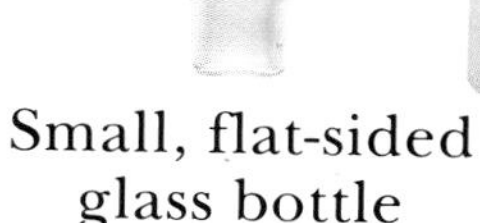

Small, flat-sided glass bottle

Smooth wooden board

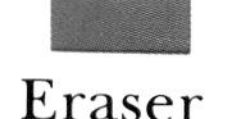

Eraser

Wooden block

The glass bottle slides down first. Its smooth sides move easily over the board.

1 Place the objects in a line at one end of the board. Then slowly lift this end of the board.

The eraser is the last object to move. Its rubbery surface creates strong friction with the tilting board.

The rough pumice stone creates more friction than the glass bottle and slides more slowly.

The smooth wooden block slides down the board quite easily.

2 Keep on lifting the board. The objects begin to move one after the other.

Keep on rolling

Find out how friction builds up when you add weight to an object. Then see how you can make movement easier by reducing friction with rollers.

You will need:

Used match

Rubber band

Sticky tape

Scissors

Pebbles

Round colouring pencils

Cardboard box

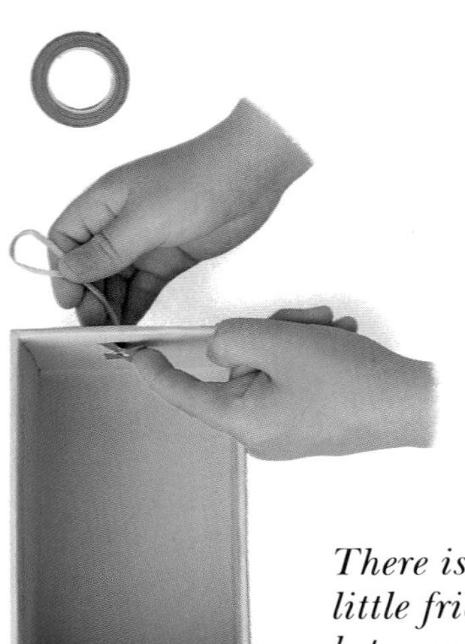

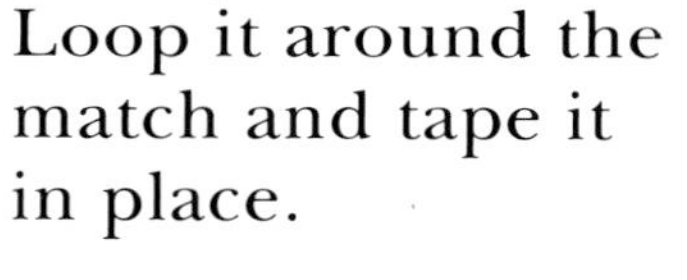

1 ⚠ Cut a small hole in one end of the box. Push the rubber band through the hole. Loop it around the match and tape it in place.

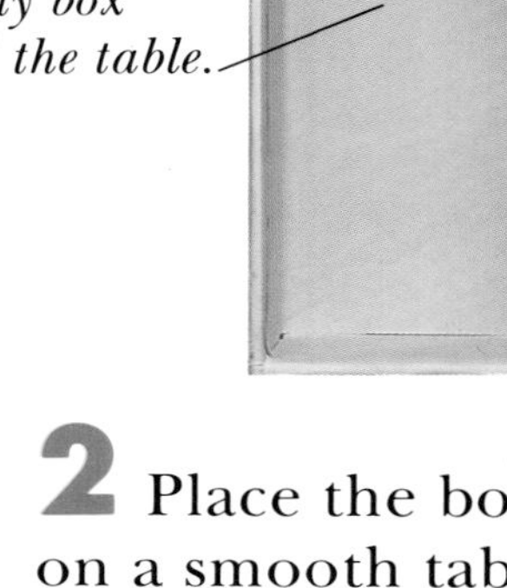

There is very little friction between the empty box and the table.

2 Place the box on a smooth table. Pull the rubber band. The box moves easily.

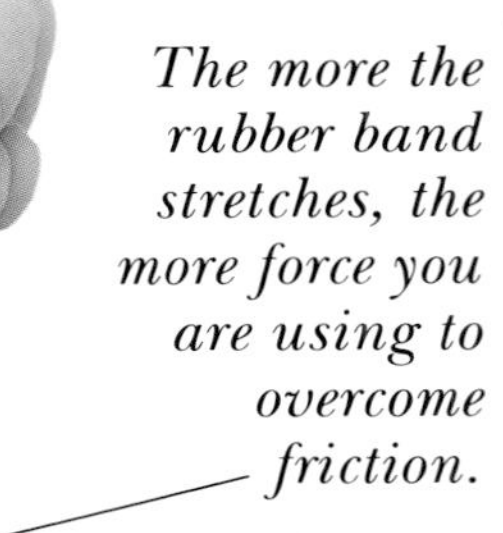

The heavier the box, the greater the friction.

The more the rubber band stretches, the more force you are using to overcome friction.

3 Fill the box with pebbles and pull again. The rubber band stretches before the box moves.

4 Now place a line of colouring pencils on the table and lay the heavy box on top.

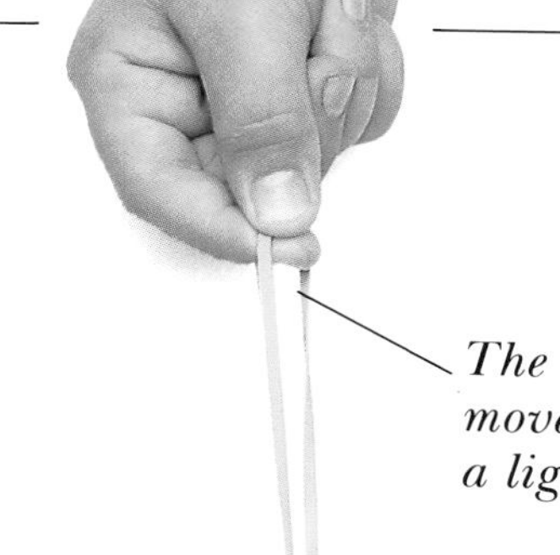

The heavy box moves with just a light pull.

The pencils act as rollers. They reduce the friction between the box and the table.

5 Pull the rubber band again. This time the heavy box rolls on the pencils and moves easily.

Smooth ride

Have you ever ridden down a giant slide? You sit on a mat that reduces the amount of friction between your body and the surface of the slide. With less friction, you slide really fast.

Swinging record

Spin a record on a string and see how strangely a spinning object moves. It stays steady as it spins and never wobbles about.

You will need:

String

Card

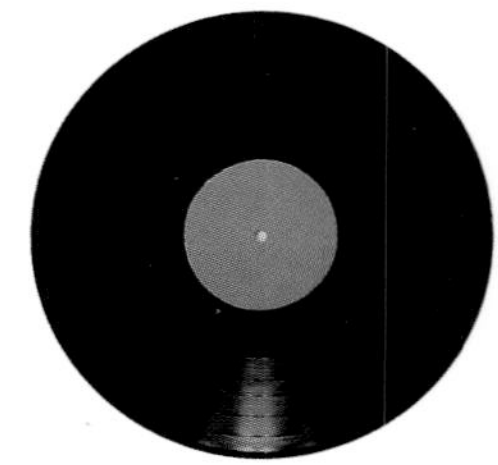

Pencil

LP record

1 ⚠ Using the point of the pencil, make a small hole in the centre of the card.

2 Tie a knot in one end of the string. Thread the other end through the hole in the card.

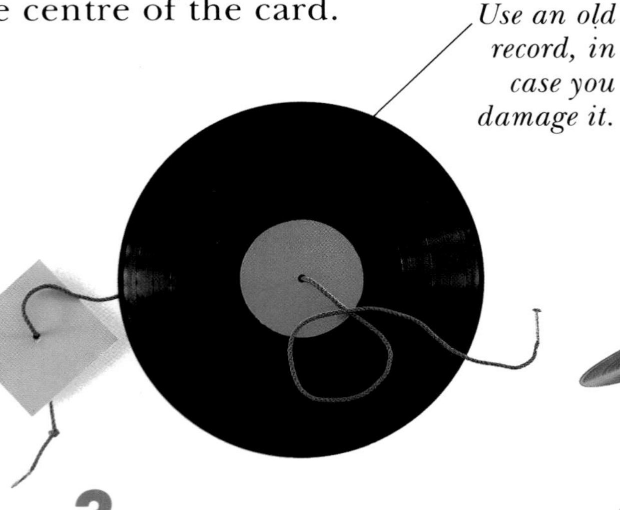

Use an old record, in case you damage it.

3 Thread the string through the hole in the record.

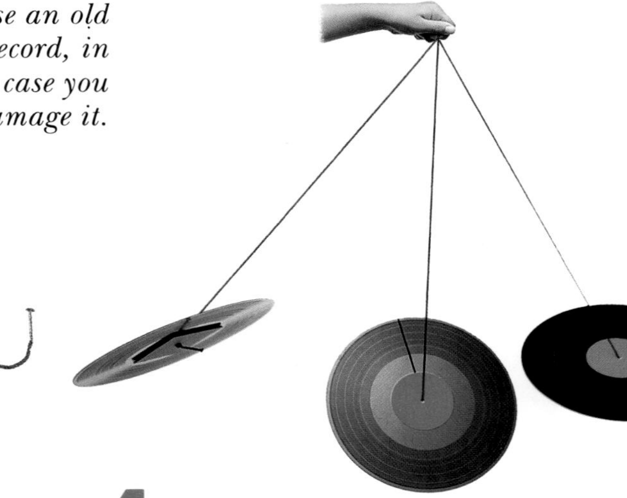

4 Hold the record by the string and swing it to and fro. It tilts in different directions.

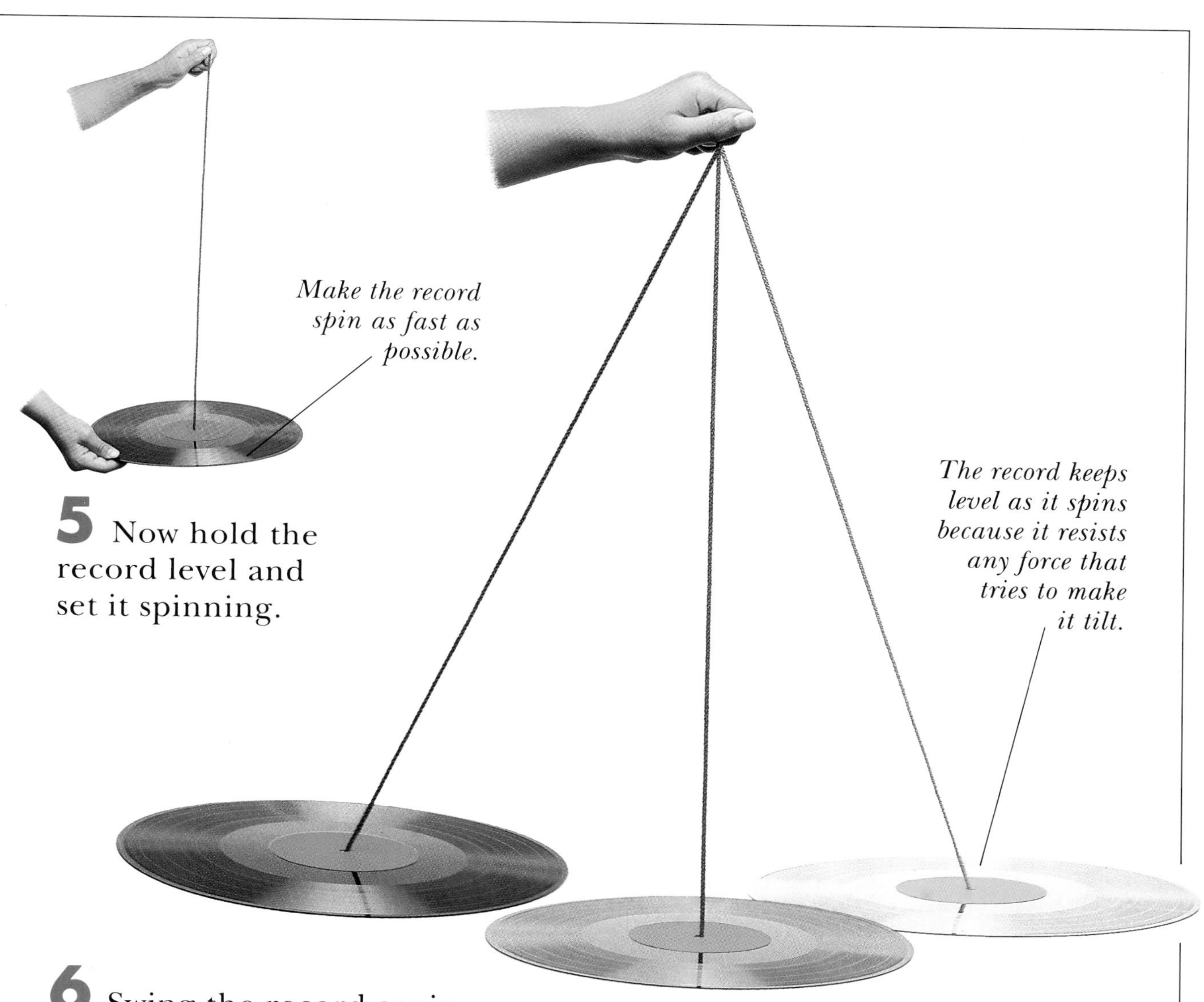

5 Now hold the record level and set it spinning.

6 Swing the record again. This time it keeps level and does not tilt.

Travelling on two wheels
You have to be moving on a bicycle to keep it upright. The spinning wheels resist the tilting that happens if the bicycle begins to fall over. This helps the wheels stay upright as you ride along.

Wail of a time

Make a wailing whirler that never stops moving. You can keep it going by pulling on its strings at just the right moment.

You will need:

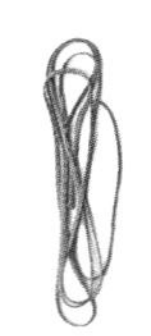

String

Compasses with pencil

Scissors

Strong card

Bendy straw

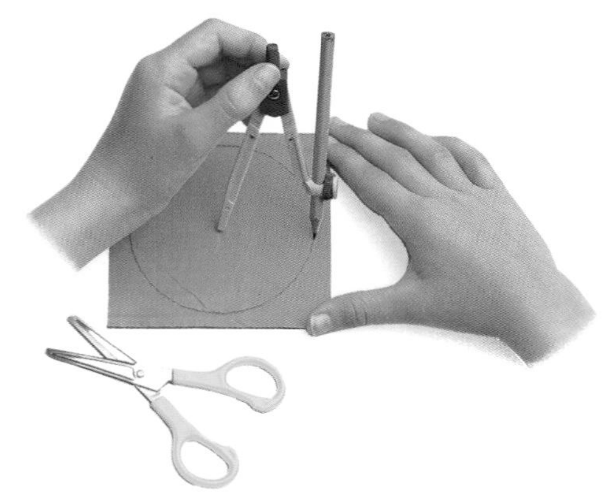

1 Use the compasses to draw a circle about 10 cm across on the card. Cut it out. This is your disc.

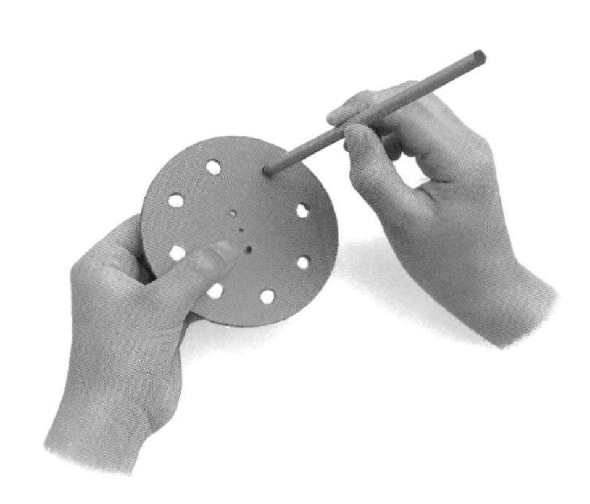

2 ⚠ Make eight big holes around the edge of the disc with the pencil. Put two small holes either side of the centre.

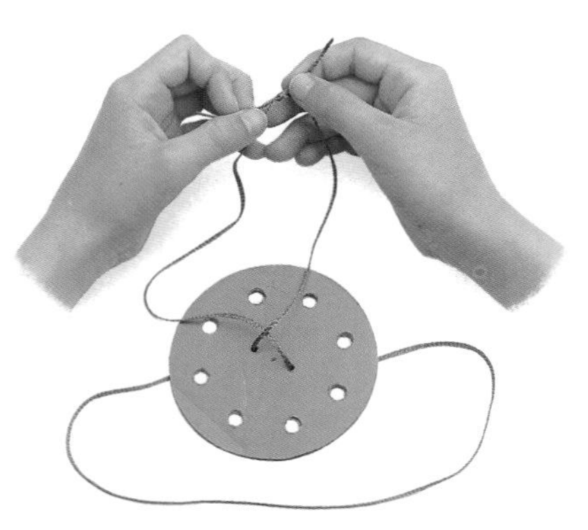

3 Thread the string through the two holes in the middle of the disc and tie the ends together.

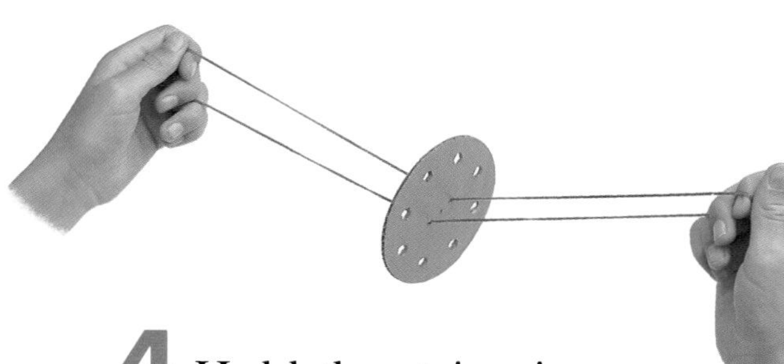

4 Hold the string in both hands. Swing the disc round to wind up the string.

5 The disc whirls round as the string winds and unwinds. To keep the disc whirling, give a quick pull with both hands just as the string winds right up to your fingers.

With each pull of the string, you add a force that speeds up the disc again.

The changing speed of the disc makes the sound go up and down like a wail.

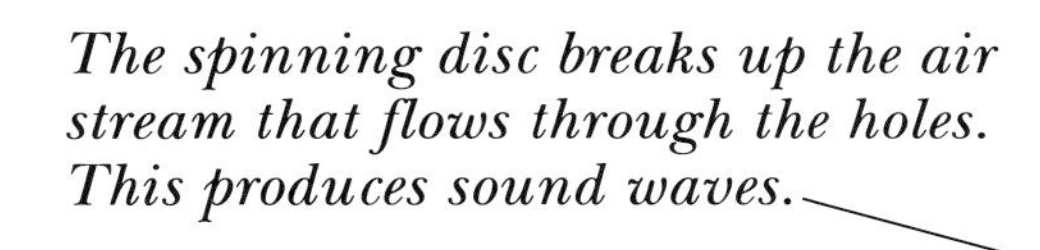

The spinning disc breaks up the air stream that flows through the holes. This produces sound waves.

6 Bend the straw. Then blow a stream of air on to the holes in the spinning disc. It makes a strange wailing noise!

Getting in the swing

Do you know how to keep a swing moving? As you reach the top of your swing, pull on the ropes or push on the seat. This adds force to the swing and keeps its movement going.

Loop the loop

How do you get dried peas to stay in a cup that turns upside-down? If you spin the cup round in a circle, the peas' inertia keeps them from falling out.

You will need:

Bendy straw

Plasticine

Two short lengths of string

Dried peas

Cotton reel

Scissors

Plastic cup

Sticky tape

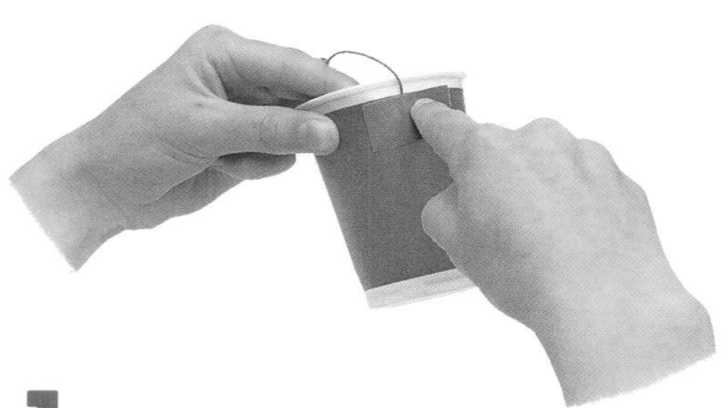

1 Tape one length of string to the cup to form a handle.

Secure the string with some tape.

2 Using the other length of string, tie the handle of the cup to the long part of the straw.

3 Push the short part of the straw through the cotton reel. Fix the plasticine over the end of the straw to hold it in place.

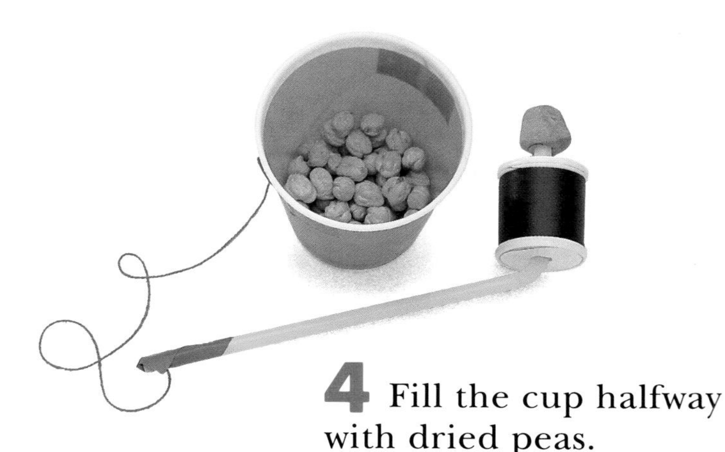

4 Fill the cup halfway with dried peas.

5 Hold the cotton reel and swing the cup in a circle. The peas do not fall out, even though the cup turns upside-down!

As the cup spins round, the peas' inertia makes them try to move upwards and outwards. This keeps the peas in the cup.

Thrills, not spills
Inertia helps to keep the passengers in their seats as the cars turn completely upside-down on this exciting roller coaster.

Picture credits
(Picture credits abbreviation key: B=below, C=centre, L=left, R=right, T=top)

Allsport: 15BR; Allsport/Jon Nicholson: 6CL; Allsport/Mike Powell: 14BL, 25BR; J. Allan Cash: 23BR; Bruce Coleman/Bob and Clara Calhoun: 7TR; Colorsport: 12BR; Lupe Cuhna: 29CL; The Image Bank/Alain Choisnet: 7TL; The Image Bank/Paul Katz: 7CL; The Image Bank/Peter M. Miller: 6B; The Image Bank/Bernard Roussel: 11BL; Camilla Jessel: 27BL; Pictor International: 17BR, 19BL; Science Photo Library/Roger Ressmeyer, Starlight: 9BR

Picture research Clive Webster
Science consultant Jack Challoner
Additional photography Dave King and Tim Ridley

Dorling Kindersley would like to thank Jenny Vaughan for editorial assistance; Basil Snook for supplying toys; Mrs Bradbury, Mr Millington, the staff and children of Allfarthing Junior School, Wandsworth, especially Natasha Aitken, Richard Clenshaw, Ashley Giles, Francesca Hopwood Road, Matthew Jones, Kemi Owoturo, Casston Rogers-Brown, and Ben Sells.